AN IMAGINATION LIBRARY SERIES

WORLD'S LARGEST

SNAKES

African Rock Pythons

by Valerie J. Weber

Please visit our web site at: www.garethstevens.com
For a free color catalog describing Gareth Stevens Publishing's
list of high-quality books and multimedia programs,
call 1-800-542-2595 (USA) or 1-800-387-3178 (Canada).
Gareth Stevens Publishing's fax: (414) 332-3567.

Library of Congress Cataloging-in-Publication Data available upon request
from publisher. Fax (414) 336-0157 for the attention of the Publishing
Records Department.

ISBN 0-8368-3652-9

First published in 2003 by
Gareth Stevens Publishing
A World Almanac Education Group Company
330 West Olive Street, Suite 100
Milwaukee, WI 53212 USA

Text: Valerie J. Weber
Cover design and page layout: Scott M. Krall
Series editor: Jim Mezzanotte
Picture Researcher: Diane Laska-Swanke

Photo credits: Cover © John Cancalosi/naturepl.com; p. 5 © Gerald & Buff Corsi/Visuals
Unlimited; p. 7 © Ferrero-Labat/Ardea London Ltd.; pp. 9, 13 © Joe McDonald/Visuals
Unlimited; pp. 11, 15, 19 © Bruce Davidson/naturepl.com; p. 17 © Peter Blackwell/naturepl.com;
p. 21 © Ake Lindau/Ardea London Ltd.

Printed in the United States of America

1 2 3 4 5 6 7 8 9 07 06 05 04 03

Front cover: **An African rock python slips easily through tight spaces. It can move across many kinds of surfaces.**

TABLE OF CONTENTS

Words that appear in the glossary are printed in **boldface** type the first time they occur in the text.

Africa's One Giant Snake

Many movies show Africa as a land crawling with giant snakes. In these movies, a huge snake is always startling explorers by **lunging** from a tree or from the **underbrush**. But there's only one real giant snake in Africa — the African rock python.

African rock pythons can grow to a length of 25 feet (7.6 meters). They live south of the Sahara Desert in the southern part of the African **continent**.

Open wide! Like other snakes, an African rock python can open its mouth so wide that it can swallow meals larger than its head.

A Brown and Black Beauty

An African rock python is usually light brown and covered with splotches that are the color of coffee. Black lines surround these dark splotches. A mark in the shape of an arrow covers most of the top of its head.

Most African pythons in their natural **habitats** grow to between 13 and 20 feet (4 and 6 m) long. At zoos, rock pythons measuring 15 or 16 feet (4.6 to 4.9 m) long can weigh up to 120 pounds (54 kilograms).

An African rock python slips almost silently through grass, across rocks, and under bushes. Many strong muscles work separately to move it along.

Keeping a Constant Temperature

In the early morning, an African rock python **slithers** out from under its rock and suns itself in the heat of a new day. Later in the day, when the Sun has risen high in the sky and the temperature is very hot, the rock python will glide into the shade of a bush.

Like other reptiles, snakes are **cold-blooded**. They rely on the temperature outside their bodies to stay warm. An African rock python moves from warm sunlight to cool shade or water to keep its body at about the same temperature.

In the forest, an African rock python soaks up heat from a log in sunlight. Later, the snake will have to find a cooler spot.

Room to Grow

African rock pythons molt, or shed their skin, as they grow — and they never stop growing! Molting replaces worn-out skin and helps heal injuries quickly.

When a snake gets ready to molt, its eyes become cloudy for a short time because they are covered with skin, too. The snake cannot see as well as it usually does, so it is more likely to be in danger from **predators**. It usually goes into hiding until it has finished shedding.

An African rock python rubs against the ground or on rocks to help remove its old skin. A snake's skin is brightest after it molts.

Like most snakes, African rock pythons get very cranky when they are about to molt. They may even attack if they are disturbed.

A Variety of Homes

African rock pythons live all over southern Africa, except in the desert, where the snakes would not have enough shade for protection against the Sun. They glide through grasslands, forests, farmlands, and mountains, and they often swim in the waters of lakes, swamps, and rivers.

Sometimes rock pythons stay in another animal's **burrow** to escape the heat of the Sun. They also climb trees or stay underwater near the banks of a stream to lie in wait for their **prey** to pass.

Younger and smaller African rock pythons can climb through the trees. As they get older and bigger, they become too heavy to climb the higher, thinner branches.

Hunting by Heat

An African rock python tracks its prey by sensing body heat. **Organs** near its lips and nostrils sense the difference in temperature between the prey's body heat and the air temperature. By moving its head back and forth to test the temperature in different places, the rock python can figure out the exact location of its prey.

In the trees, an African rock python's prey includes birds, monkeys, and other creatures living in the branches. On the ground, it feeds on pigs, small apes, antelopes, jackals, and other animals.

Giant snakes often hunt at night. The snakes' heat-sensing organs help them find prey even when it is very dark.

When's Dinner?

All giant snakes can wait a long time between meals, but the African rock python can wait for an amazing amount of time. It can go without eating for more than two years!

When the rock python does eat, however, it eats a lot. A 16-foot (5-m) African python was once found with a 130-pound (60-kg) gazelle inside it. This kind of meal shows up as a big lump in the snake's body. A rock python might need several days to **digest** its prey completely.

This Thompson's gazelle is still alive, but it may not be for long. The African rock python could squeeze the animal to death in minutes.

A Help to Farmers

Like all snakes, the African rock python can help people by keeping down the number of **pests**. Homes and farms would have a lot of rodents such as mice and rats without snakes around gobbling them down.

African rock pythons have not lived in the East Cape region of South Africa since 1927. Lately, however, farmers have brought the snakes back to the region to feed on cane rats. These pests eat the farmers' sugarcane and corn.

When a snake swallows its prey, it starts with the animal's head first. The snake uses a lot of spit to ease the prey down its throat.

Dangerous People

The African rock python's most dangerous predators are people. Some people hunt the rock python for its meat, while others want its beautiful skin to make handbags and shoes.

Parts of the African rock python are also used to make traditional medicines. The snake's skin and **spine**, for example, are supposed to help people who have skin trouble or back problems.

These pythons are also in danger from **pollution** and from the loss of their habitats as people build farms, homes, and roads in the areas where the snakes live and hunt. Collectors also hunt African rock pythons to keep or sell as pets.

A giant African rock python can weigh up to 250 pounds (113 kg). Unfortunately, some people want its skin to make handbags and shoes!

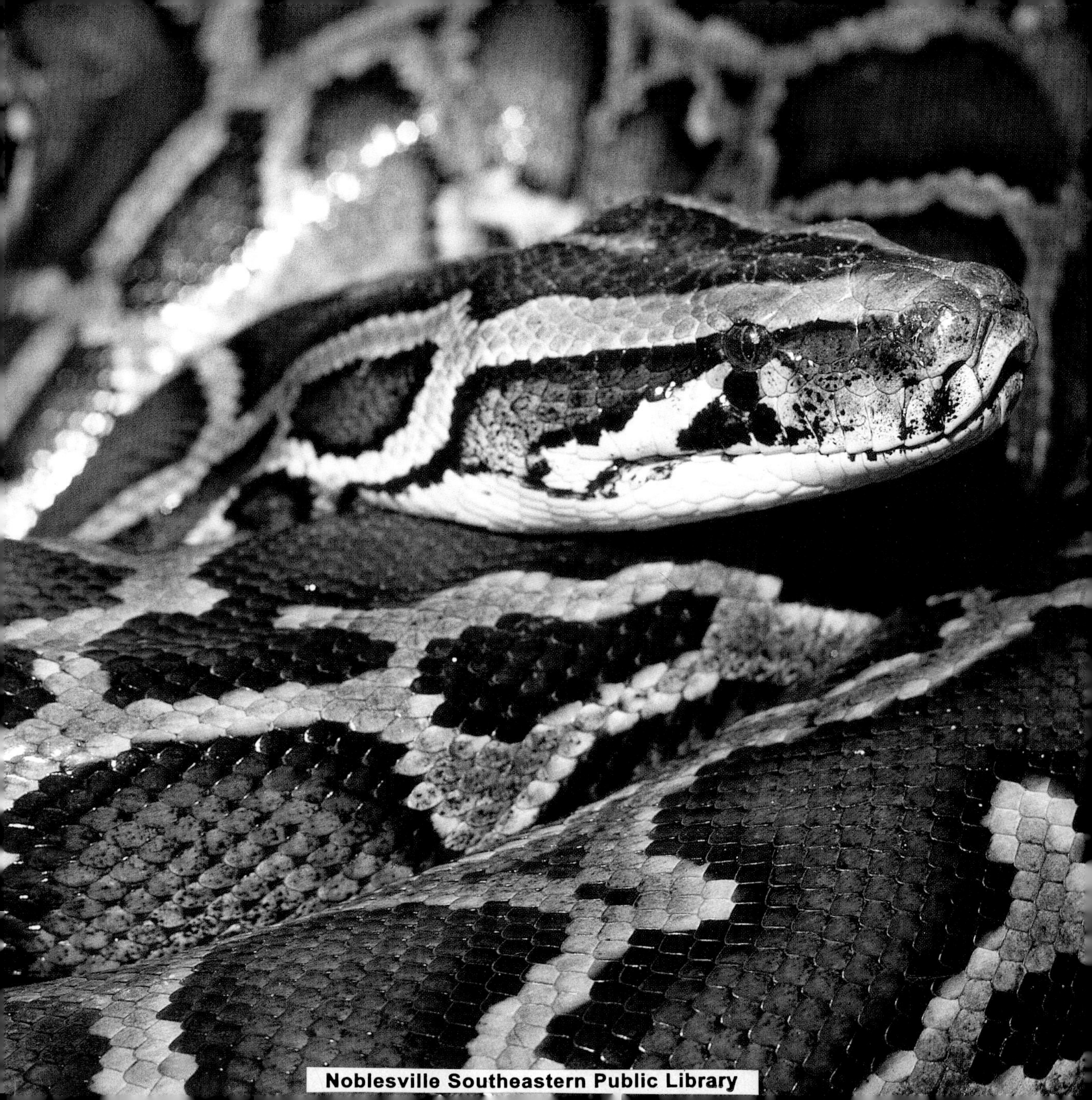

MORE TO READ AND VIEW

Books (Nonfiction) *Fangs!* (series). Eric Ethan (Gareth Stevens)
Pythons. Animal Kingdom (series). Julie Murray (Abdo & Daughters)
Pythons. Animals & the Environment (series). Mary Ann McDonald
(Capstone Press)
Pythons. Naturebooks (series). Don Patton (Child's World)
Pythons. Really Wild Life of Snakes (series). Doug Wechsler
(Rosen Publishing Group)
Pythons. Snakes (series). James E. Gerholdt (Checkerboard Library)
Pythons and Boas: Squeezing Snakes. Gloria G. Schlaepfer and
Mary Lou Samuelson (Franklin Watts, Inc.)
Snakes. Seymour Simon (Bt Bound)

Books (Fiction) *How Snake Got His Hiss.* Marguerite W. Davol (Orchard Books)
I Need a Snake. Lynne Jonell (Putnam Publishing Group)
Snake Camp. George Edward Stanley (Golden Books)

Videos (Nonfiction) *Animal Life for Children: All About Reptiles.* (Schlessinger Media)
Fascinating World of Snakes. (Tapeworm)
Predators of the Wild: Snake. (Warner Studios)
Snakes: The Ultimate Guide. (Discovery Home Video)

PLACES TO WRITE AND VISIT

Here are two places to contact for more information:

Black Hills Reptile Gardens
P.O. Box 620
Rapid City, SD 57709
USA
1-800-355-0275
www.reptile-gardens.com

Great Lakes Aquarium
353 Harbor Drive
Duluth, MN 55802
USA
1-218-740-3474
www.glaquarium.org

Oregon Zoo
4001 Sun Canyon Rd.
Portland, OR 97221
USA
1-503-226-1561
www.zooregon.org

WEB SITES

Web sites change frequently, but we believe the following web sites are going to last. You can also use good search engines, such as **Yahooligans!** [www.yahooligans.com] or Google [www.google.com], to find more information about African rock pythons. Here are some keywords to help you: *African rock pythons, African snakes, pythons, reptiles,* and *snakes.*

www.enchantedlearning.com/subjects/ reptiles/snakes/Pythonprintout.shtml
Visit this site to learn how African rock pythons hunt and what they eat. Print the line drawing of the African rock python, color it in, and hang it on your wall. Then you can tell your friends all you know.

www.glaquarium.org/victoria/python.html
African rock python is from the web site hosted by the Great Lakes Aquarium. On this page, see a photograph of an African rock python and learn how it catches its prey.

www.goafrica.co.za/joburg/july_2002/ snake.stm
African rock pythons are in the news! *Joburg* is the official web site for the city of Johannesburg, South Africa. Learn how the city's zoo is taking part in a project to study and preserve the African rock python. See photographs of this fascinating snake!

www.congogorillaforest.com/ r-africarockpyth.html
Visit this web site to see a close-up photograph of an African rock python's head. Learn about the snake's size and color, as well as the threats it faces from both animals and people.

www.zooregon.org/Cards/Primates/snake. python.african.rock.htm
African Rock Python is from the web site hosted by the Oregon Zoo. This page has many facts about the African rock python, including the snake's size, eating habits, and habitat.

GLOSSARY

You can find these words on the pages listed. Reading a word in a sentence helps you understand it even better.

burrow (BURR-oh) — a hole in the ground that an animal uses for shelter 12

cold-blooded (kold BLUD-id) — having a body temperature that changes with the temperature of the air outside 8

continent (CONT-in-unt) — one of the seven large areas of land on Earth 4

digest (dye-JEST) — to break down food in the mouth and stomach so it can be used for energy 16

habitats (HAB-uh-tatz) — places where an animal or plant lives 6, 20

lunging (LUNJ-ing) — moving forward in a very sudden way 4

organs (OR-gunz) — parts in the body that do a particular job 14

pests (PESTZ) — animals or plants that cause problems for people 18

pollution (puh-LOO-shun) — waste created by people that is harmful to animals and the environment 20

predators (PRED-uh-turz) — animals that hunt other animals for food 10, 20

prey (PRAY) — animals that are hunted by other animals for food 12, 14, 16, 18

slithers (SLITH-urz) — moves by sliding 8

spine (SPYNE) — the backbone of an animal or person, which is formed by a series of bones that are joined together 20

underbrush (UN-der-brush) — plants such as bushes that grow beneath large trees 4

INDEX